Illinois

BY AMY VAN ZEE

The Child's World

Published by The Child's World®
1980 Lookout Drive • Mankato, MN 56003-1705
800-599-READ • www.childsworld.com

ACKNOWLEDGMENTS
The Child's World®: Mary Berendes, Publishing Director
The Design Lab: Design and production
Red Line Editorial: Editorial direction

PHOTO CREDITS: Noel Powell/Schaumberg/Shutterstock Images, cover, 1, 3; Matt Kania/Map Hero, Inc., 4, 5; Eugene Moerman/Shutterstock Images, 7; Steve Geer/iStockphoto, 9, 11; iStockphoto, 10; Lisa F. Young/iStockphoto, 13; Photolibrary, 15; Jim Jurica/iStockphoto, 17; AP Images, 19; Nagel Photography/Shutterstock Images, 21; One Mile Up, 22; Quarter-dollar coin image from the United States Mint, 22

LIBRARY OF CONGRESS CATALOGING-IN-PUBLICATION DATA
Van Zee, Amy.
  Illinois / by Amy Van Zee.
     p. cm.
  Includes bibliographical references and index.
  ISBN 978-1-60253-457-5 (library bound : alk. paper)
  1. Illinois—Juvenile literature. I. Title.

F541.3.V36 2010
977.3—dc22

2010016164

Printed in the United States of America in Mankato, Minnesota.
July 2010
F11538

On the cover:
Many people enjoy the rides at Navy Pier in Chicago, Illinois.

CONTENTS

Geography

Let's explore Illinois! Illinois is in the central United States. This area is called the Midwest. Lake Michigan is on the northeast border of Illinois. It is one of the Great Lakes.

WISCONSIN

Lake
Michigan

MICHIGAN

IOWA

• Galena

• Rockford

Evanston •
• Chicago

Joliet •

• Moline

• LaSalle

ILLINOIS

• Peoria

Danville •

INDIANA

Petersburg •

Mississippi River

Springfield

MISSOURI

• Alton

• Collinsville

• Olney

Ohio River

NORTH
WEST
EAST
SOUTH

KENTUCKY

Cities

Springfield is the capital of Illinois. Chicago is the state's largest city. Chicago lies along the banks of Lake Michigan. Rockford and Peoria are other large cities in the state.

Lake Michigan is one of the five Great Lakes. The other four are Lake Erie, Lake Huron, Lake Ontario, and Lake Superior.

Chicago is one of the largest cities in the United States. ▶

Land

The Mississippi River makes up the western border of Illinois. The Ohio River is part of the southern border. Much of Illinois is flat. This land is called **plains**. There are some hills and valleys in the north. Much of the soil in Illinois is good for growing crops.

Wildflowers grow on the Illinois plains. ▶

Plants and Animals

The Illinois state tree is the white oak.
Wood from the white oak can be used to
make furniture. The state flower is the
purple violet. The state bird is the cardinal.
Male cardinals are bright
red. Females are often
brown and red.

The white oak has gray **bark**. ▶

People and Work

Almost 13 million people live in Illinois. Many people work in hotels, restaurants, and stores. Some people work in **finance** and **insurance**. Farmers grow corn, soybeans, and wheat. Other people work in **manufacturing**.

Illinois produces many dairy products, such as milk. Chickens, turkeys, and hogs are raised in Illinois, too.

Some people who work in manufacturing make machines. ▶

History

Native Americans have lived in the Illinois area for thousands of years. In the 1600s, fur traders from France traveled along the Mississippi River and explored Illinois. The Illinois **Territory** was created in 1809. Illinois became the twenty-first state on December 3, 1818.

Fur trading was a common way to make a living until the 1800s. ▶

Ways of Life

Many people in Illinois live in or near large cities. People enjoy shopping and visiting **museums**. Many people visit Lake Michigan, where they can boat, fish, and swim.

People enjoy a Chicago beach during a warm Illinois summer. ▶

Famous People

U.S. Secretary of State Hillary Rodham Clinton grew up in Illinois. Writer Ernest Hemingway was born in the state. He won awards for his stories. Carl Sandburg was from the state, too. He wrote the well-known **poem** "Chicago."

Abraham Lincoln, the sixteenth president of the United States, lived most of his life in Illinois. Illinois is sometimes called "the Land of Lincoln."

As secretary of state, Hillary Rodham Clinton ▶ travels to many countries to speak to their leaders.

Famous Places

Chicago is home to Willis Tower. It is the tallest building in the United States. It used to be named Sears Tower. In Springfield, visitors can see the house where Abraham Lincoln lived for 17 years.

Lincoln's home in Springfield was built in 1839. ▶

State Symbols

Seal

The Illinois state seal shows a bald eagle. The bald eagle is the national bird. Go to childsworld.com/links for a link to Illinois's state Web site, where you can get a firsthand look at the state seal.

Flag

The seal is on the state flag. The flag became the official Illinois flag in 1970.

Quarter

Abraham Lincoln is on the Illinois state quarter. The quarter came out in 2003.

ILLINOIS

Glossary

bark (BARK): Bark is the covering on a tree trunk. The white oak, the Illinois state tree, has gray bark.

finance (FYE-nanss): Finance is a group of businesses that take care of money. Some people in Illinois work in finance.

insurance (in-SHUR-unss): Insurance is something people can buy to help them with money in case of an accident. Insurance is a large industry in Illinois.

manufacturing (man-yuh-FAK-chur-ing): Manufacturing is the task of making items with machines. Manufacturing is important in Illinois.

museums (myoo-ZEE-umz): Museums are places where people go to see art, history, or science displays. Illinois has many museums.

plains (PLAYNZ): Plains are areas of flat land that do not have many trees. Illinois has many plains.

poem (POH-um): A poem is a piece of writing that often has short lines and sometimes rhymes. Carl Sandburg, who grew up in Illinois, wrote a well-known poem.

seal (SEEL): A seal is a symbol a state uses for government business. The bald eagle is shown on the Illinois seal.

symbols (SIM-bulz): Symbols are pictures or things that stand for something else. The seal and flag are symbols for Illinois.

territory (TAYR-uh-tor-ee): A territory is a piece of land that is controlled by another country. The Illinois Territory was formed in 1809.

Further Information

Books

Blanton, Lynne, and Betsy Hedberg. *States*. Lincolnwood, IL: Publications International, 2002.

Dennis, Yvonne Wakim, and Arlene Hirschfelder. *A Kids' Guide to Native American History*. Chicago, IL: Chicago Review Press, 2010.

Wargin, Kathy-jo. *L is for Lincoln: An Illinois Alphabet*. Chelsea, MI: Sleeping Bear Press, 2000.

Web Sites

Visit our Web site for links about Illinois: *childsworld.com/links*

Note to Parents, Teachers, and Librarians: We routinely verify our Web links to make sure they are safe and active sites. So encourage your readers to check them out!

Index